People Who Need People

PEOPLE WHO

A Book About Friendship

NEED PEOPLE

Selected by Barbara Loots

Illustrated by Frances Yamashita

♛ HALLMARK EDITIONS

People Who Need People

You're the greatest.
The very best
to you always
Sharon

July 1975

My Friend

I love you not only for what you are,
but for what I am when I am with you.

I love you not only for what you have made
of yourself, but for what you are making of me.

I love you because you have done more than any creed
could have done to make me good, and more
than any fate could have done to make me happy.

You have done it without a touch,
without a word, without a sign.

You have done it by being yourself. Perhaps
that is what being a friend means, after all.

ROY CROFT

The Wine of Friendship

In his book CREATIVE LIVING FOR TODAY
author Maxwell Maltz ponders the importance
of friendship in the world. His conclusion:
"Life without friendship is like cereal without milk."

You turn the dial of your radio; it lights up and out comes music.

The music may be sweet and melodious; it may be harsh and jangling.

But, usually, one theme underlies it. The longing for love—for friendship.

The lyrics may be sensitive or trite; they may be lovely or moronic; they may be Cole Porter sophistication or unimaginative vulgarity.

Still, no matter how crude, they are verbalizations of the agonizing human need for love—for friendship.

If we penetrate the many disguises under which the friendship instinct operates, we come to a fundamental human need which our communication media so headline: *the need for deep friendship between people*....Life without friendship is like cereal without milk; there can be no sense of completion. Real friendship is a subtle, trusting interrelationship whose worth is too great to be measured.

In the words of America's first President, George Washington, "Be courteous to all, but intimate with few, and let those few be well tried before you give them your confidence. True friendship is a plant of slow growth, and must undergo and withstand the shocks of adversity before it is entitled to the appellation."

Another great President, Thomas Jefferson, once compared friendship to wine.

Yes, like good wine, friendship can give you a lift.

Like wine, it lasts. Inclement conditions do not destroy it.

And, as Jefferson points out, it is "restorative"; it renews a person grappling with life's problems, refreshing him so that, given a good night's sleep, he can call once again upon his resources to go toward the battles of life.

Friendship is a treasure.

It is a fundamental ingredient in the cooking pot of the delicious dish that is creative living.

A Friend in Need

"A friend in need," my neighbor said to me,
"A friend indeed is what I mean to be;
In time of trouble I will come to you,
And in the hour of need you'll find me true."

I thought a bit, and took him by the hand:
"My friend," said I, "you do not understand
The inner meaning of that simple rhyme;
A friend is what the heart needs all the time."

HENRY VAN DYKE

My Kind of Friends

Many aspects of friendship are universal,
as revealed by this description of "good friends"
by the Chinese author Lin Yutang.

I want some good friends, friends who are as familiar as life itself, friends to whom I need not be polite, and who will tell me all their troubles, matrimonial or otherwise, who can quote Aristophanes and crack some dirty jokes, friends who are spiritually rich and who can talk dirt and philosophy with the same candor, friends who have definite hobbies and opinions about persons and things, who have their private beliefs and respect mine.

The more I travel the more I realize that fear makes strangers
of people who should be friends. SHIRLEY MACLAINE

If You Want A Friend, Tame Me...

In Antoine Saint- Exupéry's story "THE LITTLE PRINCE,"
a small visitor from a distant planet lands
on the earth and travels in search of understanding.
This conversation between the little prince
and a fox he meets shows in a charming
yet profound way how friends are discovered—
and what true friendship can mean.

"Good morning," said the fox.

"Good morning," the little prince responded politely.

"Who are you?" asked the little prince, and added, "You are very pretty to look at."

"I am a fox," the fox said.

"Come and play with me," proposed the little prince. "I am so unhappy."

10

"I cannot play with you," the fox said. "I am not tamed."

"Ah! Please excuse me," said the little prince.

But, after some thought, he added:

"What does that mean—'tame'?"

"It is an act too often neglected," said the fox. "It means to establish ties."

"'To establish ties'?"

"Just that," said the fox. "To me, you are still nothing more than a little boy who is just like a hundred thousand other little boys. And I have no need of you. And you, on your part, have no need of me. To you, I am nothing more than a fox like a hundred thousand other foxes. But if you tame me, then we shall need each other. To me, you will be unique in all the world. To you, I shall be unique in all the world....

"If you tame me, it will be as if the sun came to shine on my life. I shall know the sound of a step that will be different from all the others. Other steps send me hurrying back underneath the ground. Yours will call me, like music, out of my burrow. And then look: you see the grainfields down yonder? I do not eat bread. Wheat is of no use to me. The wheat fields have nothing to say to me. And that is sad. But you have hair that is the color of gold. Think how wonderful that will be when you have tamed me! The grain, which is also golden, will bring me back the thought of you. And I shall love to listen to the wind in the wheat...."

The fox gazed at the little prince, for a long time.

"Please—tame me!" he said.

"I want to, very much," the little prince replied. "But I have not much time. I have friends to discover, and a great many things to understand."

"One only understands the things that one tames," said the fox. "Men have no more time to understand anything. They buy things all ready made at the shops. But there is no shop anywhere where one can buy friendship, and so men have no friends any more. If you want a friend, tame me...."

Compliment Unmeant

Compliments are a natural part of friendship.
Phyllis McGinley considers the friendly compliment from
a new angle—and sheds an amusing light on the subject.

Among my souvenirs are a few oblique pieces of
adulation. As the stamp fancier cherishes his
errata—the issues printed upside down, the
blurred specimens quickly withdrawn from cir-
culation—so I value the flawed compliment. In
fact, I consider it the cream. Very dear indeed is
the comment of an old friend, offered to me a
number of years ago. She was a good deal older
than I, so I leaned on her as one would on a kindly
aunt, knowing that she believed me, however
wrongheadedly, to be comely, clever and destined
for high places. The one thing of which she could
not convince me was that I owned a brilliant and

bewitching smile. I knew only too well that, having been brought up on the Colorado prairies, where orthodontists did not exist, I would never qualify in a contest for Miss Ipana. "But, Phyllis," she told me dreamily one day, "you have *fascinating* teeth. They're so individual—no two alike." That friend has gone on to more flowery places, where she is no doubt consoling some angel whose harp has come untuned, with the assurance that dissonances are always interesting.

While Such Friends Are Near Us

Those are red-letter days in our lives when we meet people who thrill us like a fine poem, people whose handshake is brimful of unspoken sympathy and whose sweet, rich natures impart to our eager, impatient spirits a wonderful restlessness which, in its essence, is divine.

The perplexities, irritations and worries that have absorbed us pass like unpleasant dreams, and we wake to see with new eyes and hear with new ears the beauty and harmony of God's real world. The solemn nothings that fill our everyday life blossom suddenly into bright possibilities.

In a word, while such friends are near us we feel that all is well. Perhaps we never saw them before and they may never cross our life's path again; but the influence of their calm, mellow natures is a libation poured upon our discontent, and we feel its healing touch as the ocean feels the mountain stream freshening its brine.   HELEN KELLER

Throw Away Your Blinders!

Too often we choose our friends only from our own social and economic strata—to the exclusion of all others. Writer Vance Packard long ago discovered that interesting and rewarding friendships can be found everywhere. He urges us to open our eyes to the possibilities.

Some people contend that we are happiest when we stick to "our own kind" in developing friendships. The person who wears blinders of this sort will never experience the enthrallment of having as companions such colorful and often vividly articulate individuals as clam diggers, house detectives, lumberjacks, seamen or antique refinishers. He'll never know the exhilaration that comes from the discovery of someone exciting in a seemingly unlikely place.

I confess that when I first left college I took a similar attitude toward people outside my tiny world. As a "hardened" young newspaperman in New York City I was rather proud that I didn't know a single person in the apartment house where my bride and I lived. One day my father and mother came to visit the Big City. The very first morning I found Dad chatting animatedly with the doorman. As I hurried Dad away, he said, "You know, he's from Bellefonte. He thinks he played football against you."

Later that morning I took Dad and Mother on a sight-seeing tour to Staten Island. On the boat trip Mother sat down beside a dark-complexioned girl and soon was chatting excitedly with her. Again I was mortified. Afterward, Mother told me that the girl was a medical student from Kenya and had been explaining to her some of Kenya's hair-raising problems in coping with yaws, sleeping sickness and leprosy. Tactfully I tried to suggest to my parents that in New York one does not chat with people one does not know. Dad asked, "Why not?" My mouth opened, but no good answer would come out. Only then did it dawn on me that I, like many other people, had harnessed myself with blinders.

Since then I have had the good fortune, partly because of my work, to be thrown with a great variety of people: high-altitude window washers, zoo keepers, heads of state, junk dealers, divorce lawyers, gold miners, movie stars, lonely multi-millionaires, Vermont carpenters. Their differentness, I've found, gives them an infinite capacity to fascinate — and to broaden one's personal horizon.

Miscellaneous File

Just why should friends be chronological,
Fraternal friends, or pedagogical,
Alike in race or taste or color—
  It only makes the meetings duller!
Unclassified by tribe or steeple,
Why shouldn't friends be merely people?

DOROTHY BROWN THOMPSON

Recipe for Friendship

Common interest is the basis for many a friendship.
Here Sylvia Fine Kaye, wife of entertainer Danny Kaye,
tells how her famous husband launched
his avocation as a gourmet cook—
and cooked up a pretty good friendship as well.

In spite of his intense interest and curiosity about food, he gave absolutely no sign of becoming a cook. As a matter of fact, one of his chief occupations at home was looking helpless. No one ever dreamed of asking him to raise a window shade, fix a faucet, or boil an egg. If there was nobody in the kitchen when he got home, he would open the refrigerator, stare hopefully at the food until it wilted, then close the door, and go upstairs hungry. Not until the summer of 1955, that is, when we ate our way from Paris to the south of France.

Claude Terrail, owner of La Tour d'Argent in Paris, had provided the reservations, which were

all but impossible at last-minute notice—which is Danny's style. Accompanied by two close friends, with the intrepid redhead at the wheel of a bad-tempered, overused Chevrolet, we stopped first at the town of Saulieu where Alexandre Dumaine, King of French Chefs, reigned. And I use the verb advisedly. No one, but *no* one was permitted in his kitchen, including his wife. When Joseph Wechsberg did a three-part *New Yorker* profile on Dumaine, Wechsberg was allowed to stand in the doorway, and not a step nearer.

We were told this on arrival when Danny asked Madame D. if he could go in and see the Maître. When Danny said he had a personal message for him, Madame said she would try to coax him out after his nap. At five in the afternoon he reluctantly appeared—an imposing figure of enormous girth, starched from hat to foot, with red cheeks, a black moustache, and polite eyes. He was totally taken aback when, on introduction, Danny leaped up and kissed him on both cheeks saying, "This is from Claude Terrail, and this from M. La Serre." Slightly disarmed, Monsieur

Dumaine sat down for a moment. He asked what we would like for dinner. Danny said, "Whatever you would like us to eat." The eyes got warmer. He then asked what time we would like dinner. Danny asked, "What time would you *like* us to have dinner?" With his brown eyes now twinkling, the Maître thundered to Madame, "Champagne!" We had a superb dinner, deceptively simple, with a matchless Montrachet.

Afterward, Monsieur Dumaine not only came out to the little bar (a rare occurrence) but sat with us for two hours. The fact that Danny spoke little French and Dumaine no English was no deterrent—they became instant friends. Neither did he have the faintest idea of who Danny was or what he did. That the word had gotten round and the little bar was bursting at the seams with movie fans while others peered in through the windows made no dent whatever. After all, he was Dumaine, the greatest chef in France. Way past his usual bedtime when he bade us farewell, there were tears in his eyes, and he and Danny embraced each other fervently.

To My Friend

Because you are my friend
I long today
To bring you some imperishable gift
Of beauty.
Something glowing and warm
Like the coals of living fire,
Something as cool and sweet
As lilies at dawn,
Something as restful and clean
As smooth white sheets at night
When one is very tired,

Something with the taste of spring water
From high places,
Or like the tang of cool purple grapes
To the mouth.
But O my friend,
Since I cannot buy such gifts for you,
Come go with me
Out into the little everyday fields of living,
And let us gather in our baskets, like manna,
God's gift to us:
The down-pouring, exquisite beauty
Of life itself.

GRACE NOLL CROWELL

Definitions

FRIEND:

1. Anybody who listens instead of argues.
2. One who is always thinking of you,
   when all others are thinking of themselves.
3. A person who knocks before he enters,
   not after he has taken his departure.
4. One who comes in when the whole world
   has gone out.
5. A present you give yourself.
6. A speaking acquaintance who also listens.
7. Somebody you don't have to talk to.
8. Someone you can count on to count on you.
9. Someone who runs interference for you
   in your pursuit of happiness.

WILLIAM B. FRANKLIN

My Friend Carl Sandburg

*Journalist Harry Golden was for many years a close
friend of the great American poet Carl Sandburg.
Here Golden pays eloquent tribute to that friendship.*

My friendship with Carl Sandburg was the most rewarding of my life. Carl was all-out for friendship. If Carl was your friend and your son was sick, Carl worried as much as you. If you were depressed, Carl wanted to share your depression as he wanted to share your exhilaration when you were happy. Carl, as a friend, accepted your entire universe, every star, jungle, and person in it.

On Sandburg's eighty-fifth birthday, William Jovanovich, the publisher of Harcourt, Brace, gave him a splendid party honoring the publication of *Honey and Salt*, Carl's last book of poems. Justice William O. Douglas was there, Eric Johnston, John Steinbeck, Barbara Tuchman, John Gunther, Marian Anderson, Elia Kazan, Herbert

Mitgang, S. L. A. Marshall, and many others, all of them close to Carl.

Carl Sandburg said to me, "Harry, it's a dream come true. I got me a big room, and it's all filled with my friends. Happens once in your life."

from My Friend

"He is my friend!" The words
Brought summer and the birds;
And all my winter-time
Thawed into running rhyme
And rippled into song,
Warm, tender, brave, and strong.

And so it sings to-day.—
So may it sing always!
Let each mute measure end
With "Still he is thy friend."

JAMES WHITCOMB RILEY

A Little Girl's Mark Twain

Children often make the best friends of all because
they are completely honest, open and innocent.
Mark Twain knew this, and that is why he so often
wrote about children. The following story is the
true account of how a little girl captured the great
writer's heart and started a wonderful friendship. It was
written by Dorothy Quick — that very same little girl.

A little girl walked round and round the deck of
an ocean liner. On the starboard side she fairly
flew along, but when she turned the corner and
came to the port side of the vessel, she walked
slowly and her feet dragged, her eyes lost in admiration of a man who stood at the rail, talking to
another man. Both of them were staring out towards the far horizon line, and didn't see the little
girl, whose gaze was riveted on the older of the

29

two, the one with a great shock of snowy white hair and a keen, kindly observant face. He was Mark Twain.

I can still remember the thrill I had when, after walking past him five or six times, he suddenly turned, held out his hand and said in a slow, drawly voice, "Aren't you going to speak to me, Little Girl?" His companion faded away into space, as far as I was concerned, when I took his place. In a few seconds I was at the rail, standing beside the Mark Twain whom only yesterday I had seen walking down the platform of a London station surrounded by literally hundreds of admirers. He hadn't seen me hanging half out of the compartment window to catch a glimpse of him, nor had I at that moment dreamed that the next morning I should be standing beside him on the deck of a steamer bound for New York—standing beside him and actually talking to him.

Almost before I knew it, Mr. Clemens had arranged to have his steamer chair by ours, and I discovered that without doubt I had made a new friend. That night, as usual, I wore a white sailor suit to dinner. Being only nine, I had my dinner very early, so I didn't see Mr. Clemens; but just as I was getting into bed there was a knock on the door and it was my new friend clad in one of his famous white suits, come to see me in mine! Someone had told him about my costume.

Unfortunately, I was attired in pajamas so I could only promise, as he especially requested, to wear the white sailor suit the next day. Fortunately, I had a large supply of them, for he insisted I wear them throughout the rest of the voyage. So we both appeared each day in white. Mark Twain's were made of white flannel and mine of serge, but everyone assured us that we looked very well together....

We were inseparable for the rest of the voyage; he literally wouldn't let me out of his sight. All the papers made much of our friendship. "Mark Twain Home—Captive of Little Girl" was one of the headlines. And they carried long paragraphs about me. I have them all and with them another souvenir of the trip, a drawing of Buster Brown with sprouting wings looking at the following: "RESOLVED, that Mark Twain has deserted the entire ship's company for Dorothy Quick. I wish my name was Twain. Buster." This is pasted in my scrapbook....

On the dock, my new friend and I parted. But this was the beginning of a treasured friendship, which was for me a great privilege and joy.

To Friendship

A friend is someone lovely, who
Cuts her chrysanthemums for you
And, giving, cares not for the cost,
Nor sees the blossoms she has lost;
But rather, values friendship's store,
Gives you her best and grows some more.

ELEANOR LONG

The Character of a Friend

The poetic character sketches of poet Edwin Arlington
Robinson teach valuable lessons about living.
"Cliff Klingenhagen" is a small glimpse into the life
of a man who demonstrates the happiness to be found
in forgetting one's self for the sake of a friend:

Cliff Klingenhagen had me in to dine
With him one day; and after soup and meat,
And all the other things there were to eat,
Cliff took two glasses and filled one with wine
And one with wormwood. Then, without a sign
For me to choose at all, he took the draught
Of bitterness himself, and lightly quaffed
It off, and said the other one was mine.

And when I asked him what the deuce he meant
By doing that, he only looked at me
And grinned, and said it was a way of his.
And though I know the fellow, I have spent
Long time a-wondering when I shall be
As happy as Cliff Klingenhagen is.

A Genius for Friendship

*In this warmly personal account, American writer
Katherine Anne Porter describes her friend Sylvia Beach,
who had not only the gift of making friends,
but also the overwhelming desire to share her gift
and its joys with everyone.*

When I first saw her, in the early spring of 1932, her hair was still the color of roasted chestnut shells, her light golden brown eyes with greenish glints in them were marvelously benign, acutely attentive, and they sparkled upon one rather than beamed, as gentle eyes are supposed to do. She was not pretty, never had been, never had tried to be; she was attractive, a center of interest, a delightful presence not accountable to any of the familiar attributes of charm. Her power was in the unconscious, natural radiation of her intense energy and concentration upon those beings and arts she loved.

Sylvia loved her hundreds of friends, and they all loved her—many of whom loved almost no

35

one else except perhaps himself—apparently without jealousy, each one sure of his special cell in the vast honeycomb of her heart; sure of his welcome in her shop with its exhilarating air of something pretty wonderful going on at top speed. Her genius was for friendship; her besetting virtue, generosity, an all-covering charity in its true sense; and courage that reassured....

As I say, Sylvia's friends did not always love each other even for her sake, nor could anyone but Sylvia expect them to, yet it is plain that she did. At parties especially, or in her shop, she had a way, figuratively, of taking two of her friends, strangers to each other, by the naps of their necks and cracking their heads together, saying in effect always, and at times in so many words, "My dears, you *must* love one another."

It is said that we do not make our friends, that we simply recognize them.   FAITH BALDWIN

The Influence of Friendship

*Did we think that friendship is merely
a one-for-one arrangement? Georgia Luccock Schmitt
shows how friendship between just two people
can have an effect on all of life.*

Think for a bit of the people whom you know and of their effect upon you; those to whom you are particularly drawn; those who for no apparent reason at all seem to irritate you and "rub you the wrong way"; those who draw out the most irresponsible, carefree side of your nature, or who stimulate and waken the very worst; those whose presence make of life a beautiful thing and stir within you impulses to fuller, nobler living. Then realize that you are having an equally important effect upon all with whom you may come in contact. Into the hands of every individual is given a marvelous power for good or ill, for sowing either beauty or unsightly weeds within the great Garden of Life. Each hour that you spend with a   37 friend leaves both you and that individual a different person, living on either a higher or a lower plane, for psychologists tell us that even an hour's conversation will lift or lower the level of life. Even more, you are, in an hour's visit, changing in some measure the lives of people whom you will never know or see. Just as the perfume which you give your friend is worn by her, carrying its fragrance into lives you will never know, so also is the contagion of your character transmitted through your friend to others whom you will never meet. The influence of friendship is radiated from one person to another in endless and incalculable degree.

Friends are our windows on the world.   WILL OURSLER

What Men Live By

Russian author Leo Tolstoy once wrote a brief allegory in which an Angel disguised as a man is sent to earth by God to learn these three lessons: what is given to men, what is not given to men, and what men live by. At the conclusion of the story, the Angel reveals his identity to the poor shoemaker who had taken him in, and speaks of the lessons he has learned.

The clothes fell off the body of the Angel, and he was clothed with light so that no eye could bear to look upon him, and he began to speak more terribly, as if his voice did not come from him, but from Heaven. And the Angel said:

"I learnt that man does not live by care for himself, but by love for others. It was not given the mother to know what was needful for the life of her children; it was not given to the rich man to know what was needful for himself; and it is not given to any man to know whether by the evening he will want boots for his living body or slippers for his corpse. When I came to earth as a man, I

lived not by care for myself, but by the love that was in the heart of a passerby, and his wife, and because they were kind and merciful to me. The orphans lived not by any care they had for themselves; they lived through the love that was in the heart of a stranger, a woman who was kind and merciful to them. *And all men live, not by reason of any care they have for themselves, but by the love for them that is in other people.*

"I knew before that God gives life to men, and desires them to live; but now I know far more. I know that God does not desire men to live apart from each other, and therefore has not revealed to them what is needful for each of them to live by himself. He wishes them to live together united, and therefore has revealed to them that they are needful to each other's happiness."

Give of yourself, give as much as you can....
If everyone were to do this and not be as mean with
a kindly word, then there would be much more
justice and love in the world.   ANNE FRANK

Ira

In her autobiography DAYBREAK, *Joan Baez describes
the beginning of her friendship with Ira Sandperl,
a friend who helped to shape her ideas about life.*

I met Ira when I was sixteen. My father was still
taking us to Quaker meetings.... There I was, sixteen, squirming through the Sunday morning
silences and occasionally teaching the kindergar-
ten class.

One sunny but boring Sunday, as I recall now,
there was a funny bearded man at the meeting-
house, and he had a laugh like a goat. He smiled
and laughed lots, and his eyes were always filling
with tears. He was some kind of legendary person,
because most of the kids already knew him. I
heard he was going to take over our high school
first-day classes. That's all I can remember about
the first time I met Ira—that it was sunny, and
that he had a laugh like a goat.

He did take our class, and we began to call his

sessions the "sermons on the pavement." He talked a lot about Gandhi, and something called non-violence, and we read from a book by a Chinese philosopher named Lao-tse. One of the things Lao-tse said was, "The is is the was of what shall be," and I thought that that was the cleverest thing I'd ever heard.

I began to grow very fond of the bearded guru with the goat laugh. I felt he might have answers that no one else had.

Ira dressed in corduroys and sweatshirts and a baggy duffle coat and a beat-up Alpine hat. He began to come by my house on his bicycle every morning before school. I'd skip first period and he'd be late to work, and we'd walk in the morning sun and make jokes about the world, and at the same time I knew that he and I felt desperately that we must do something to try and help the world.

We travel together, teach together, march together, laugh and cry together, sit-in together, and

go to jail together. He is an endless joy to me....
It has been a spiritual marriage which has brought
only the most constructive...companionship.

Riches

I have never been rich before,
But you have poured
Into my heart's high door
A golden hoard.

I look for no greater prize
Than your soft voice.
The steadiness of your eyes
Is my heart's choice.

I have never been rich before,
But I divine
Your step on my sunlit floor
And wealth is mine!

ANNE CAMPBELL

Friendship Between Women

On friendship between women, author Jessamyn West writes,
"...the woman who is happiest in her relationship
with men is richest in her friendships with women."

Why should it be otherwise? Friendship, like love, implies a relationship; and as in most arts, aptitude in related fields. The men who have celebrated masculine friendship—Montaigne, Boswell, Keats—did not do so as lovers of sour grapes or as foxes without tails. All were devoted to and impassioned about women. Is masculine and feminine biology so different? What is the essence of friendship, anyway?...

When the possibility of friendship between women is as taken for granted as women's relationship with God and man,...Woman will then write, as Montaigne did, not of friendship but of a friend. She will begin her piece, as I shall begin my next, "For forty years I had a friend whose name was Carmen Cook."

Communication Becomes Communion

In this reflection from her book A GIFT FROM THE SEA, *Anne Morrow Lindbergh tells us that even silence between friends can be a form of communication.*

At home, when I meet my friends in those cubby-holed hours, time is so precious we feel we must cram every available instant with conversation. We cannot afford the luxury of silence. Here on the island I find I can sit with a friend without talking, sharing the day's last sliver of pale green light on the horizon, or the whorls in a small white shell, or the dark scar left in a dazzling night sky by a shooting star. Then communication becomes communion and one is nourished as one never is by words.

Charms on the Bracelet of Life

What's more fun than to be at a party with all your friends around you! Friends make life happy—they are life's greatest treasure. Here writer Marjorie Holmes talks about the beauty of friendship and how it can make us more beautiful ourselves.

It was a party, in the truest sense of the word. An assortment of interesting people, small enough so that strangers could become acquainted, old friends could talk. Yet large enough to be full of laughter and music and pleasantries and stimulating new contacts.

On impulse I remarked to our hostess, Peg Howe: "You certainly have a lot of lovely friends."

"Oh, yes," she laughed. And lifting her braceleted arm she remarked, "My friends are the charms on my bracelet of life."

The charms! I thought. Why—yes. The enhancements, the adornments—that extra shining something. If you truly love and enjoy your

friends they are a part of the golden circlet that makes life good.

When you gather them about you, you feel happy—and proud. Their accomplishments add a glow to your own being. What's more, you want to share them: "He's a distinguished surgeon, and his wife makes a home for all these foreign students—you must meet them...." "They both do little theater work, you'll just love them, they're

both so alive—" "...He plays folk songs on the guitar and sings in three languages—" "...Now that the children are in school she's studying law...."

But not only their accomplishments, their qualities: "Helen is the most generous person I've ever known...." "Grace has the most beautiful brown eyes—when she talks they just shine—" "...Jim has a laugh that makes you feel good all over. And you can depend on what he says, he'd never let you down—"

The person who can feel and speak this way about his friends is truly blessed. His life is rich in meaningful relationships. His "friends" are not a source of criticism and carping and jealousy and gossip. They are people truly dear to him, so dear that he can't refrain from singing their praises to others. And in so doing he is always making new ones. For the way a person feels about his friends is a pretty accurate indication of the kind of person he or she is.

The man or woman who treasures his friends is usually solid gold himself.

The World Is Full of Beauty

The world is full of beauty—
Sparkling seas,
A garden in full bloom,
The shape of trees,
A child's eyes dancing
With some new delight,
A sky ablaze with stars
All twinkling bright,
A sun-splashed meadow's gold,
The rainbow's end...
But more than these— the love
Of friend for friend.

KATHERINE DAVIS

Opposites Attract

*Friendship is not always based on a similarity
of interests or of temperament. In her memoirs
Lillian Hellman warmly remembers and describes her friend,
the late Dorothy Parker.*

It was strange that we did like each other and that
never through the years did two such difficult
women ever have a quarrel, or even a mild, unpleasant word. Much, certainly, was against our
friendship: we were not the same generation,
we were not the same kind of writer, we had led
and were to continue to lead very different lives,
often we didn't like the same people or even the
same books, but more important, we never liked
the same men.

If she denounced everybody else, I had a right to think that I was included, but now I think I was wrong about that, too: so many people have told me that she never did talk about me, never complained, never would allow gossip about me, that I have come to believe it. But even when I didn't, it didn't matter. I enjoyed her more than I have ever enjoyed any other woman. She was modest—this wasn't all virtue, she liked to think that she was not worth much—her view of people was original and sharp, her elaborate, overdelicate manners made her a pleasure to live with, she liked books and was generous about writers, and the wit, of course, was so wonderful that neither age nor illness ever dried up the spring from which it came fresh each day.

If a man could mount to Heaven and survey the mighty universe, his admiration of its beauties would be much diminished unless he had a friend to share in his pleasure.

CICERO   53

The River We Are Upon

One of Charles Dickens' closest early friendships
was with Maria Beadnell; however, the blossoming romance
was cut off by her parents and she eventually married
Henry Winter. Over twenty years later she wrote to the now
famous Dickens, who responded with the following letter.

Tavistock House,
Saturday, Tenth February 1855

I constantly receive hundreds of letters in great
varieties of writing, all perfectly strange to me,
and (as you may suppose) have no particular interest in the faces of such general epistles. As I
was reading by my fire last night, a handful of
notes was laid down on my table. I looked them
over, and, recognizing the writing of no private
friend, let them lie there and went back to my

book. But I found my mind curiously disturbed,

and wandering away through so many years to such early times of my life, that I was quite perplexed to account for it. There was nothing in what I had been reading, or immediately thinking about, to awaken such a train of thought, and at last it came into my head that it must have been suggested by something in the look of one of those letters. So I turned them over again—and suddenly the remembrance of your hand came upon me with an influence that I cannot express to you. Three or four and twenty years vanished like a dream, and I opened it with the touch of my young friend David Copperfield when he was in love.

There was something so busy and so pleasant in your letter—so true and cheerful and frank and affectionate—that I read on with perfect delight until I came to your mention of your two little girls. In the unsettled state of my thoughts, the existence of these dear children appeared such a prodigious phenomenon, that I was inclined to suspect myself of being out of my mind, until it occurred to me, that perhaps I had nine children

of my own! Then the three or four and twenty years began to rearrange themselves in a long procession between me and the changeless Past, and I could not help considering what strange stuff all our little stories are made of.

My Dear Mrs. Winter, I have been much moved by your letter; and the pleasure it has given me has some little sorrowful ingredient in it. In the strife and struggle of this great world where most of us lose each other so strangely, it is impossible to be spoken to out of the old times without a softened emotion. You so belong to the days when the qualities that have done me most good since, were growing in my boyish heart that I cannot end my answer to you lightly. The associations my memory has with you made your letter more—I want a word—invest it with a more immediate address to me that such a letter could have from anybody else. Mr. Winter will not mind that. We are all sailing away to the sea, and have a pleasure in thinking of the river we are upon, when it was very narrow and little.—Faithfully your friend.   57

True Friendship

What is true friendship? It is the kind of friendship that is deep enough to overcome the many misunderstandings that occur between people every day. Jewish philosopher Ben Zion Bokser writes here about just such a friendship. And he tells us how we might all enjoy the fruits of a friendship that is true.

One of my dearest friends walked off offended with me yesterday. He misjudged something I had said, and he felt that I had insulted his dignity. I hope I have corrected his impression, but the incident has left me with a troubled feeling.

Are not all human words possible of misjudgment? And is not every human relationship therefore vulnerable? I had become aware of the fact that I had been misjudged and so I was able to explain myself. How often do these misjudgments go unnoticed, producing rifts that widen? Many a friendship has died across a chasm created by an unfortunate word, a word innocently spoken but unfortunately misunderstood.

There is only one solution to avoid such mis-judgments. The love we cherish for our friends must be deeper and surer. A love that is deeper and surer will automatically furnish a more sympathetic point of view towards our friends, and its warmth will melt the frigidity which is the outcome of misunderstanding.

Old Friendship

Beautiful and rich is an old friendship,
Grateful to the touch as ancient ivory,
Smooth as aged wine, or sheen of tapestry
Where light has lingered, intimate and long.

Full of tears and warm is an old friendship
That asks no longer deeds of gallantry,
Or any deed at all— save that the friend shall be
Alive and breathing somewhere, like a song.

EUNICE TIETJENS

In Honor of Friendship

Two friends lived on adjoining lands—one alone, and the other with his wife and children. They harvested their grain and one night the man without a family awoke and looked on his sheaves stacked beside him.

"How good God has been to me," he thought, "but my friend with his family needs more grain than I." So he carried some of his store to his friend's field.

And the other, surveying his own harvest,

thought: "How much I have to enrich my life. How lonely my friend must be with so little of this world's joys."

So he arose and carried some of his grain and placed it on his friend's stack.

And in the morning when they went forth to glean again, each saw his heap of sheaves undiminished.

The exchange continued until one night in the moonlight the friends met, each with his arms filled on the way to the other's field. At the point where they met, the legend says, *a temple was built.*

FOLK TRADITION

Printed on Hallmark Eggshell Book paper.
Set in Romanee, a 20th century typeface designed
by Jan van Krimpen of Holland. Romanee was
created to accompany the only surviving italic of
the 17th century typefounder Christoffel Van Dijck.
Designed by Frances Yamashita.